MW00975337

That's Wild!

VAMPIRES CAN SWIM!

And other Strange Facts

GARY SPROTT

A Division of
Carson Dellosa Education
Educational Media
rourkeeducationalmedia.com

Before Reading: *Building Background Knowledge and Vocabulary*

Building background knowledge can help children process new information and build upon what they already know. Before reading a book, it is important to tap into what children already know about the topic. This will help them develop their vocabulary and increase their reading comprehension.

Questions and Activities to Build Background Knowledge:

1. Look at the front cover of the book and read the title. What do you think this book will be about?
2. What do you already know about this topic?
3. Take a book walk and skim the pages. Look at the table of contents, photographs, captions, and bold words. Did these text features give you any information or predictions about what you will read in this book?

Vocabulary: *Vocabulary Is Key to Reading Comprehension*

Use the following directions to prompt a conversation about each word.

- Read the vocabulary words.
- What comes to mind when you see each word?
- What do you think each word means?

Vocabulary Words:
- *aquatic*
- *camouflage*
- *crustaceans*
- *invertebrates*
- *molts*
- *offspring*

During Reading: *Reading for Meaning and Understanding*

To achieve deep comprehension of a book, children are encouraged to use close reading strategies. During reading, it is important to have children stop and make connections. These connections result in deeper analysis and understanding of a book.

 Close Reading a Text

During reading, have children stop and talk about the following:

- Any confusing parts
- Any unknown words
- Text to text, text to self, text to world connections
- The main idea in each chapter or heading

Encourage children to use context clues to determine the meaning of any unknown words. These strategies will help children learn to analyze the text more thoroughly as they read.

When you are finished reading this book, turn to the next-to-last page for After Reading Questions and an Activity.

Table of Contents

Wet and Wild

Dragons, bats, blobs, and vampires! It sounds like a scary movie. But it's just a sprinkling of the world's weird and wonderful water-dwelling creatures.

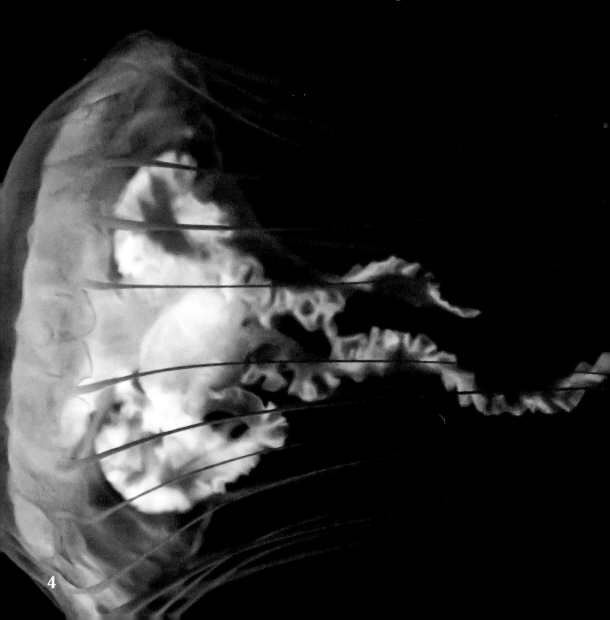

A Watery World

Water covers 71 percent of Earth. Nearly all of it is the salt water of the world's ocean, which is divided into five regions: Arctic, Atlantic, Indian, Pacific, and Southern.

It looks like a bubblegum bubble with a bad cold. The blobfish lives below the waves of the South Pacific around Australia. It grows up to 12 inches (30.5 centimeters) long and feeds by sucking up **crustaceans**. And, yes, it's kind of gross-looking!

 crustaceans (kruh-STAY-shuhns): sea creatures that have an outer skeleton, such as crabs, lobsters, or shrimp

The mysterious vampire squid has large eyes, so it can see at depths of 10,000 feet (3,048 meters). It generates light at the tips of its arms, possibly as a way to communicate in the dark. When in danger, the vampire squid wraps itself inside its eight webbed arms—like Count Dracula in his cape!

 aquatic (uh-KWAT-ik): living or growing in water

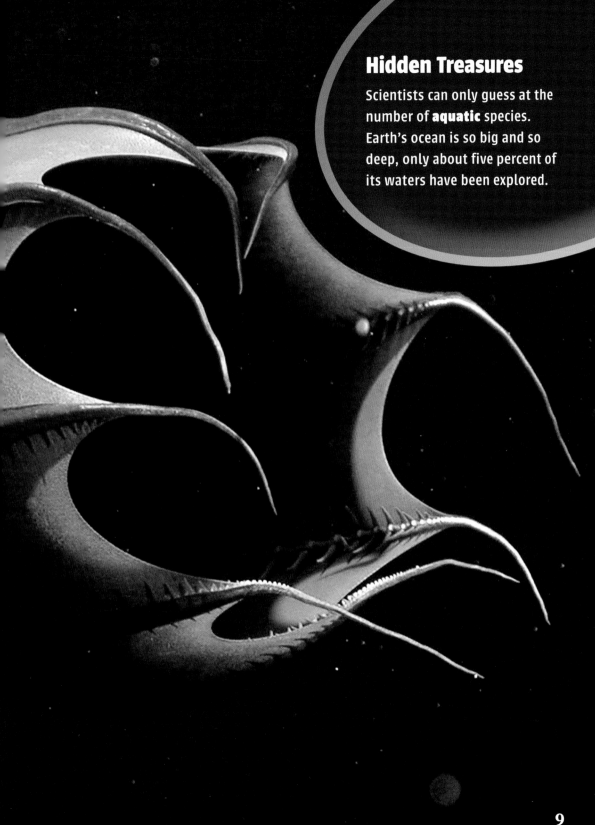

Hidden Treasures

Scientists can only guess at the number of **aquatic** species. Earth's ocean is so big and so deep, only about five percent of its waters have been explored.

Where there are vampires, there must be bats!
Batfish aren't good swimmers. But, hey, no worries.
They have thick fins that they use like legs to stroll
along the ocean floor.

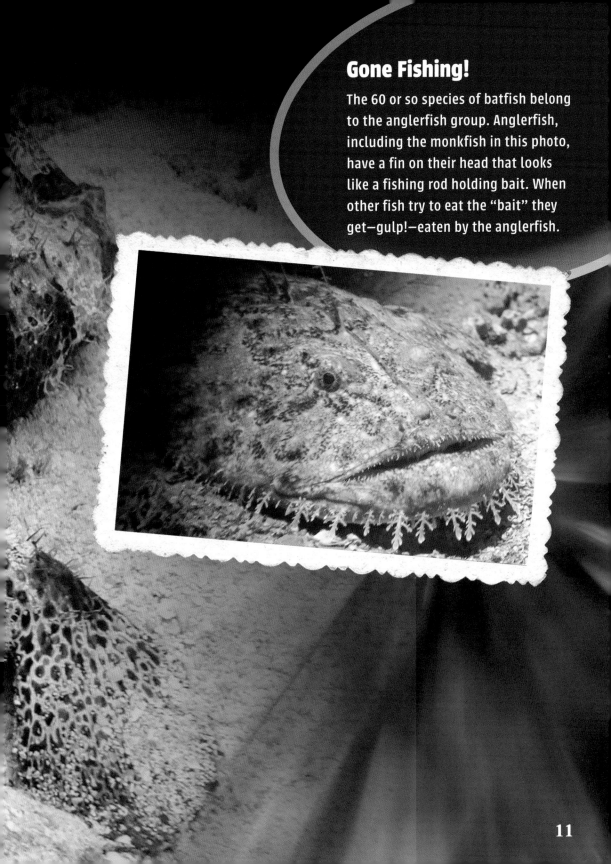

Gone Fishing!

The 60 or so species of batfish belong to the anglerfish group. Anglerfish, including the monkfish in this photo, have a fin on their head that looks like a fishing rod holding bait. When other fish try to eat the "bait" they get—gulp!—eaten by the anglerfish.

In the Amazon River of South America, there's a snake-like predator that could make your hair stand on end—literally! The electric eel can shock its prey with more than 600 volts of electricity. Whoa, that's enough to topple a horse!

Spitting Image

Female electric eels can lay up to 1,700 eggs each season. The male builds a nest with its saliva—yup, a bed of spit.

13

Animal, Vegetable, Edible?

Sea cucumbers are related to starfish. These **invertebrates** look like the cucumbers you find in your local grocery store. But some species can grow up to ten feet (three meters) long. That would make a big salad!

Oh, Poop!

Sea cucumbers have a curious way of facing danger. They tighten their muscles and shoot parts of their bodies out of ... well, there's no polite way of saying this: out of their butts!

invertebrates (in-VUR-tuh-brits): animals without backbones

camouflage (KAM-uh-flahzh): coloring or covering that makes animals, people, and objects look like their surroundings

The leafy sea dragon, pardon the pun, *leaves* you shaking your head in wonder. This relative of the seahorse has foliage-like **camouflage** that lets it hide in seaweed off the coast of Australia. Its fins move through the water like tiny boat propellers.

A Little Help from Kelp

Kelp is used to manufacture many items. From salad dressing to shampoo, toothpaste to pudding, and clothing to medicine, the ingredients in the product you are using may include a dash of salty seaweed!

Many fish and marine mammals make their homes among great underwater forests of kelp. A type of seaweed, kelp can grow as high as a tall tree—up to 150 feet (46 meters). Warming ocean temperatures threaten the kelp forests, which prefer colder water.

Colossal Calves and Tiny Pinchers

It wouldn't be fair to say that blue whale calves are just chips off the old block. They are far too big! When born, these **offspring** of the world's largest animals measure up to 25 feet (7.6 meters) long and tip the scales at three tons (2,722 kilograms). That's as big as a pickup truck.

An Extra Scoop, Please!

The tongue of an adult blue whale can weigh more than an elephant. Here's some advice: Don't share your ice cream cone with a blue whale!

 offspring (AWF-spring): the babies or young of an animal

Lobsters breed just after the female **molts** and has a soft shell. Females can carry 100,000 teeny-tiny eggs. After about a year, the eggs can be seen under the female's tail, held in place by a sticky substance. It will be another 12 months or so until these tiny pinchers hatch.

 molts (mohlts): loses an outer covering of fur, feathers, or skin so a new covering can grow

Each lobster egg is the size of the head of a pin.

Clownfish are born part girl and part boy. The fancy word for that is *hermaphrodite*. If the biggest female in a group of clownfish dies, then the biggest male will turn into a female!

Booger Shield!

Trying to find Nemo? Peek around the deadly tentacles of a sea anemone. Clownfish hide near anemones. They are covered in mucus—that's right, snot—to keep them safe from the stings.

In the cold waters of the Pacific Ocean, the female deep-sea octopus gives everything for her children. The mother protects her eggs for more than four years until they hatch! The octopus doesn't eat and doesn't travel during all that time. After its babies are born, it dies.

A Sucker for Shrimp!

Frieda, an octopus at a zoo in Germany, learned to use her eight suckered arms to open jars of her favorite foods, including shrimp.

The immortal jellyfish has a bright
red stomach and is about as big as your
fingernail. But this little jelly-belly has a
remarkable ability. If injured, the jellyfish
can return to its infant stage and
recycle itself into an adult all
over again!

Memory Game

Look at the pictures. What do you remember reading on the pages where each image appeared?

Index

After Reading Questions

1. How much of Earth's surface is covered by water?
2. What protects clownfish from a sea anemone's deadly stings?
3. What do sea cucumbers do when facing danger?
4. What did Frieda the octopus learn to do?
5. What are some items in a grocery store that might contain kelp?

Activity

The next time you visit a grocery store, count how many types of fish you can buy there. Are they from freshwater rivers or saltwater oceans? How far would you have to travel from home to find these animals in their natural habitats?

About the Author

Gary Sprott is a writer in Tampa, Florida. He once swam with sharks. Thankfully, they weren't very big and they weren't very hungry. Gary once ate shark meat. He *was* very hungry.

The amazing photographs of the vampire squid (cover, pages 8 & 9) were taken by the Monterey Bay Aquarium Research Institute using a deep-diving robotic submarine in Monterey Bay.

© 2020 Rourke Educational Media

All rights reserved. No part of this book may be reproduced or utilized in any form or by any means, electronic or mechanical including photocopying, recording, or by any information storage and retrieval system without permission in writing from the publisher.

www.rourkeeducationalmedia.com

PHOTO CREDITS: Cover & Title Page ©Monterey Bay Aquarium Research Institute; Background Pg 3, 4, 6, 10, 14, 22, 28 & Cover © TassieKarin; Pg 15 & 30 © Damsea; Pg 20 & 30 ©eco2drew; Pg 23 & 30 ©NOAA; Pg 25 & 30 © JP74; Pg 26 & 30 © Kondratuk Aleksei; Pg 8 & 30 ©Monterey Bay Aquarium Research Institute; Pg 4-5 ©Marianne Purdie; Pg 5 ©Dimitrios Stefanidis; Pg 6 ©BlobSculpin_NOAANWFSC; Pg 10 ©Southeast Fisheries Science Center/NOAA; Pg 11 ©PEDRE; Pg 12 © Kseniia Mnasina; Pg 12 © Stacey Newman; Pg 14 © e2dan; Pg 16 © Kjersti Joergensen; Pg 18 ©Macrovector; Pg 18-19 ©Joe Belanger; Pg 22 ©GlobalP; Pg 24 ©ChristianNasca; Pg 28-29 ©zaferkizilkaya; Pg 29 ©Rebecca Schreiner

Edited by: Kim Thompson
Cover and Interior design by: Kathy Walsh

Library of Congress PCN Data

Vampires Can Swim! And Other Strange Facts / Gary Sprott
(That's Wild!)
  ISBN 978-1-73161-726-2 (hardcover)
  ISBN 978-1-73161-250-2 (softcover)
  ISBN 978-1-73161-738-5 (e-Book)
  ISBN 978-1-73161-750-7 (ePub)
Library of Congress Control Number: 2019932371

Rourke Educational Media
Printed in the United States of America,
North Mankato, Minnesota